Rosemary Hellyer-Jones

The body on the beach

Ernst Klett Verlag
Stuttgart · Leipzig

Contents

Before you read

a) *Look at the picture on the front of the book. Then use this list of words/phrases to help you answer these questions.*
1. What happens/Who is called when someone is found dead? 2. Why is a post-mortem important?

b) *Explain in English what these words/phrases mean.*
1. alibi; 2. fingerprints; 3. to make a confession; 4. suicide; 5. witness box

Remember: *Use the list if you need to while you are reading!*

Chapter 2
- **CID (Criminal Investigation Department)** [ˌsi:aɪ'di:] Kripo
- **detective** [dɪ'tektɪv] Kriminalbeamte(r)
- **body** ['bɒdi] *hier:* Leiche
- **case** [keɪs] Fall
- **Scene of Crime Officers (SOCO)** [ˌsi:n əv 'kraɪm ɒfɪsəz] Kriminaltechniker
- **suicide** ['su:ɪsaɪd] Selbstmord
- **post-mortem** [ˌpəʊst 'mɔ:tem] Obduktion, Autopsie
- **clue** [klu:] Spur, Hinweis

Chapter 3
- **inquiry** [ɪn'kwaɪəri] Untersuchung, Ermittlung
- **inquest** ['ɪŋkwest] gerichtliche Untersuchung (der Todesursache)
- **coroner** ['kɒrənə] Beamter, der verdächtige Todesfälle untersucht
- **court** [kɔ:t] Gericht

Chapter 4
- **Cell Site Analysis** [ˌsel saɪt ə'næləsɪs] Dienst zur Abfrage von Telefondaten

Chapter 8
- **alibi** ['ælɪbaɪ] Alibi

Chapter 9
- **fingerprint** ['fɪŋgəˌprint] Fingerabdruck
- **DNA testing** [di:en ˌeɪ 'testɪŋ] DNA Proben
- **to charge s.o. with sth.** [tʃa:dʒd wɪθ] jmd. wegen etwas anklagen
- **identity** [aɪ'dentəti] Identität
- **to make a confession** [ˌmeɪk ə kən'feʃn] ein Geständnis ablegen

Chapter 10
- **witness box** ['wɪtnəs ˌbɔks] Zeugenstand
- **jury-box** ['dʒʊəri ˌbɔks] Geschworenenbank
- **member of the jury** [ˌmembə əv ðə 'dʒʊəri] Geschworene(r)
- **to give evidence** [gɪv 'evɪdns] aussagen
- **on oath** [ɒn 'əʊθ] unter Eid
- **forensic pathologist** [fə'rensɪk pə'θɒlədʒɪst] Gerichtsmediziner(in)
- **verdict** ['vɜ:dɪkt] Urteil

1 On the cliffs

It was a day that Eve Richards would never forget, although there was nothing unusual about the way it began. She left the house before breakfast, just like she always did, and walked up Southcliff Road with Sandy, her dog. In a few minutes they got to the cliff path. From up there the views of the sea were quite fantastic, especially on a perfect day like today. It was early May, the sun was shining, and the sky was a brilliant blue. Far away in the distance Eve could see two ships, like tiny toys, on the calm blue water. There was no wind today, so all was quiet except for the call of the seagulls.

She began to think about her plans for the rest of the week. Tomorrow was her golf day – and on Friday Polly, her granddaughter, was coming for the weekend …

"Sandy! Sandy? Where have you gone? Sandy!" The big dog had disappeared. This, also, was nothing unusual, especially up here on top of the cliffs. There were rabbits here, and Sandy loved rabbits! She often left the cliff path when she thought she had smelt or even seen one, and ran away through the heather and into the bushes. Eve waited for a few minutes, but Sandy didn't come back, so she left the path herself and started to look for her.

Then she heard her. The dog was barking excitedly now, but where was she? Eve couldn't see her at first. Then, after she had found her way past a small group of young trees, she discovered her. There Sandy was, near the edge of the cliff. She was barking so hard, Eve thought the dog would go crazy.

"Sandy! Sandy, what is it?"

Eve didn't like to go too near the edge. The cliffs were high here, and dangerous. One step too far, and you might fall over the edge. It was a long way down …

cliff [klɪf] Klippe • 1 **Eve** [iːv] • 4 **up** [ʌp] hinauf, oben • 10 **except [for]** [ɪk'sept fə] abgesehen von • 11 **seagull** ['siːgʌl] Möwe • 14 **granddaughter** ['grændɔːtə] Enkelin • 17 **rabbit** ['ræbɪt] Kaninchen • 20 **heather** ['heðə] Heidekraut • 26 **edge** [edʒ] Rand

She moved carefully nearer her dog. Just before she actually got to the cliff edge, she suddenly saw what Sandy had found. She gasped in horror.

Down on the beach, at the bottom of the red cliffs, someone was lying on the pebbles – a man, or might it be a boy? She couldn't be sure. Not far from the place where he was lying, there was a motorbike – or what was left of one.

"Oh no! This is awful! Horrible! Oh, come away from there, Sandy! At once! We must call for help!"

She moved away from the cliff edge and got her mobile out. Her hands were shaking so badly, it was difficult to hold it. In the end she managed to make the 999 call.

"Felton emergency services. Fire, police or ambulance? Which service do you need?"

"Ambulance! There's been a terrible accident! I – "

"One moment, please."

Eve waited, and another voice took the call. "Ambulance service here. Your name and address?"

"Oh – er, my name is Richards. Eve Richards. 3, North View Road, Westbourne."

5 **to lie, lay, lain** [laɪ] liegen • 5 **pebble** ['peblz] Kies • 7 **motorbike** ['məʊtəbaɪk] Motorrad • 7 **left** [left] übrig (geblieben) • 14 **Felton** ['feltn] • 21 **Westbourne** ['westbɔ:n]

"… Westbourne. Right, Mrs Richards. Where are you now, and what has happened?"

"I'm up on the cliff path at Westbourne. There's been an accident. Someone has fallen off the cliffs!"

"Where exactly? Did you walk up there from the town?"

"Yes, I came up Southcliff Road. Oh dear, it may actually be quite difficult to get an ambulance up here."

"Don't worry about that. We'll probably have to send a helicopter. OK, stay where you are. You'll be seen from the air. Try not to worry, now. OK?"

"Right. Thank you. Goodbye." The shock had made Eve quite dizzy. Later, she could never quite remember what happened next. She probably just sat down on the grass and waited … The only thing she remembered was the moment when, far in the distance, the helicopter came into view. Help was coming at last.

2 Detectives on the scene

When the CID detectives, Sergeant Steven Draper and Constable David Briggs, arrived on the scene, a lot of work had already been done by the emergency services. The paramedics who had come in the helicopter had hurried to examine the young man on the beach. They had seen at once that it was too late to help him now. He was dead. Next, a police constable in uniform had been called in. She had made sure that the area around the body and the motorbike was closed. Eve Richards had been advised to go home, and the whole area at the top of the cliff had also been closed. After that, the police constable had called the CID, because she felt suspicious: How had the accident happened? There was no road at the top of the cliff, so it

1 **right** [raɪt] OK • 12 **dizzy** ['dɪzi] schwindlig • 16 **at last** [ət 'lɑ:st] endlich • 17 **sergeant** ['sɑ:dʒənt] Polizeimeister(in) • 17 **Steven Draper** [ˌsti:vn 'dreɪpə] • 18 **constable** ['kʌnstəbl] Polizeiwachtmeister(in) • 18 **Briggs** [brɪgz] • 25 **to close** [kləʊz] absperren • 28 **suspicious** [sə'spɪʃəs] misstrauisch, verdächtig

couldn't have been a traffic accident. She knew that in a case like this, where there were questions that couldn't easily be answered, the CID would have to be in charge.

Now, a whole team of 'Scene Of Crime Officers' was at work. The two CID detectives stood together near the body.

"Sad case," said Sergeant Draper. He shook his head. "Look at him –he's only a young lad! Can't be more than 18 or 19."

"Yes, it's bad," said Constable Briggs. "He had no chance, of course. If you fall off cliffs as high as these, what can you expect?"

"Certain death, Dave, that's what you can expect. Certain death! See what I mean?" Sergeant Draper looked hard at the younger detective.

"You mean – suicide?"

"Looks a bit like it. He wasn't even wearing a helmet."

"You've got a point there, Steve. It's suspicious, at least. So you really think he rode up to the top of those cliffs on his motorbike, without a helmet – and then deliberately drove it over the edge? Why would he want to do that?"

"Why? I don't know. There could be lots of reasons … But maybe that's not what happened at all … Maybe he was pushed."

Sergeant Draper turned to the officer who was examining the boy's body.

"Time of death?" he asked him. "Have you any idea?"

"I think we can be almost sure he died about twelve to thirteen hours ago. That would put the time of death at about eight or nine o'clock last night."

"Hmm. Anything else you've discovered?"

"Not much yet. Except for the broken bones and all the other terrible injuries that killed him. More will be

---

3 **to be in charge** [bi ɪn 'tʃɑ:dʒ] zuständig sein • 8 **lad** [læd] Junge, Bursche • 13 **certain death** [ˌsɜ:tn 'deθ] sicherer Tod • 13 **Dave** [deɪv] • 17 **a bit** [ə'bɪt] ein bisschen • 23 **(not) at all** [ət 'ɔ:l] überhaupt (nicht) • 25 **to turn to s.o.** ['tɜ:n tə] sich jdm zuwenden • 32 **bone** [bəʊn] Knochen • 33 **injury** ['ɪndʒəri] Verletzung

discovered at the post-mortem, of course. You know the routine. Whether he had a problem with drugs, alcohol … Might be the case."

"Right. – Let's look at the scene at the top of the cliff, Dave. See what they've found for us there."

When they got up there, they first asked one of the team what had been found near the cliff edge.

"Nothing much, I'm afraid. No tyre marks from the motorbike, but in this dry weather you wouldn't expect to see much, especially with all the heather up here. A few broken twigs on these bushes here. This seems to be the place where he went over the edge. There are a few scuff marks over here, look. And, of course, we've found twigs and bits of heather in the wheels of the motorbike."

"Right. – OK, so what else have we got up here?" Sergeant Draper looked at the other officers who were photographing the scene and looking for clues. One of them had just picked up two or three fresh cigarette ends and put them in a plastic bag. Another had found a helmet.

"Probably his," said Sergeant Draper. "Where exactly did you find it, Sue?"

"Just near that seat over there." She showed him and Constable Briggs the place. Behind a group of bushes and well away from the cliff edge, there was a small seat, just big enough for two people to sit together. Constable Briggs sat down there for a moment. "Nice view of the sea from here!" he said. "Well hidden away, too. You can't be seen here from the cliff path."

"No, that's right, Dave, you can't," said Sergeant Draper. "A perfect meeting place for lovers, don't you think?" He turned to Sue again. "Anything else near this seat? Or on it?"

"Yes, we discovered a mobile on the seat, too."

8 **tyre mark** [ˈtaɪə mɑːk] Reifenabdruck • 9 **dry** [draɪ] trocken • 11 **twig** [twɪg] Zweig • 12 **scuff mark** [ˈskʌf mɑːk] Stelle, an der die Erde aufgeraut ist • 18 **cigarette end** [ˌsɪgəˈret end] Zigarettenstummel • 25 **well away** [ˌwel əˈweɪ] mit sicherem Abstand

"Oh? Good ... So that explains why we didn't find one on the body. I'd wondered why that was."

"What could that mean?" asked Constable Briggs. "Why would he leave his mobile up here? What do you think, Steve?"

"Again, there could be lots of reasons ... But I expect we'll find out quite a lot from that mobile, anyway. If it's his, of course ..."

Just at that moment, Sergeant Draper's own mobile rang. He got it out to take the call. "Yes? – What's that? Who? – Oh, I see. – Yes, it may be. – Yes, probably. OK, thanks. Bye!"

He turned to Constable Briggs. "A Mr and Mrs Thomson have just called – and reported their son missing. The name's Jack. 18 years old. Didn't come home last night. They've just discovered his bed wasn't slept in."

"You think this is him?"

"I'm afraid it looks like it."

3 First inquiries

"Come back to the table and have another cup of tea, Bruce. It'll do you good." Mary Thomson spoke quietly. She looked at her husband. He gave no answer, but continued to stare out of the window. Then he saw a car outside.

"They're here, Mary," he said. "We'll have to let them in."

Mary Thomson went over to the window. "Are you sure it's them? They're not wearing uniform, Bruce."

"They're CID, I expect. That must be it."

"Detectives? Surely not? Oh, Bruce!" After that morning's terrible ordeal, she felt she couldn't stand much more.

Next moment the doorbell rang. They went into the hall together, and Mary opened the door.

---

12 **Thomson** ['tɒmsn] • 13 **to report s.o. missing** [rɪˌpɔ:t sʌmwʌn 'mɪsɪŋ] jdn als vermisst melden • 14 **Jack** [dʒæk] • 20 **husband** ['hʌzbənd] Ehemann • 21 **to stare** [steə] starren • 28 **ordeal** [ɔ:'di:l] Qual

"Mr and Mrs Thomson? We're from the CID. I'm Detective Sergeant Draper, this is Detective Constable Briggs. Sorry about this – it's a bad time, we know. May we come in?"

They took the two detectives into the living room.

"We won't stay long," said Sergeant Draper. "We realize it must be very painful for you, but there are some questions we have to ask you about your son Jack. Things that may help us to find out more about this terrible tragedy. About how it happened. And why. You understand?"

They both nodded.

Constable Briggs asked the first question. "There's one very important thing we're wondering about. Did you notice anything unusual about Jack recently? The way he behaved? Did he seem to be worried at all?"

They looked at each other.

"Not really," said Bruce Thomson. "What was there to worry about? Jack was doing well at sixth form college. I wouldn't say he was worried."

"Oh, I don't know, Bruce," said his wife. "Maybe he *was* worried about something. He certainly didn't seem happy! You know how difficult he was the last few weeks. Some days he hardly spoke to us! Always in a world of his own, he was. Only last week we were talking about it. Don't you remember?"

"Of course I do. But you know what teenagers can be like, Mary. Easy to get on with one day, difficult the next."

"Yes. But with Jack it was something quite new."

Sergeant Draper looked at her. "So you would admit, then, Mrs Thomson, that your son seemed unhappy – or at least, that the way he behaved over the last weeks could have meant that he was worried about something. Is that right?"

"Yes, I think so … He wasn't happy, I know that."

5 **to realize sth** ['rɪəlaɪz] sich etw bewusst sein • 8 **tragedy** ['trædʒədi] Tragödie • 13 **to notice** ['nəʊtɪs] (be)merken • 17 **sixth form college** [ˌsɪksθ fɔːm 'kɒlɪdʒ] Schule, die Schüler auf den A-level-Abschluss vorbereitet • 20 **certainly** ['sɜːtnli] bestimmt • 22 **hardly** ['hɑːdli] kaum • 29 **then** [ðen] *hier:* also

"Now wait a minute, Sergeant," said Bruce Thomson suddenly. "What are you trying to tell us? We've lost our only child. He fell off the cliffs and was killed. What difference can it make whether he was unhappy or not?"

"I'm sorry to have to explain this to you more clearly, Mr Thomson. But you must realize that we have to consider suicide as a possible cause of death."

"Suicide?" Bruce Thomson almost shouted the word. "No! Never!" Mary Thomson began to cry quietly.

"We're very sorry," said Constable Briggs. "Very, very sorry, Mrs Thomson. Mr Thomson. You can be quite sure, nobody is saying that's what happened. We just don't know. We don't know how or why this terrible thing happened. But it's our job – the job of the police – to find out. We have to consider every possibility."

6 **to consider** [kən'sɪdə] betrachten, in Erwägung ziehen • 7 **possible** ['pɒsəbl] möglich • 7 **cause of death** [ˌkɔːz əv 'deθ] Todesursache

"Tell them about Mark Crawford, Bruce," said Mary Thomson. "Maybe then they'll understand."

"Mark Crawford?" Sergeant Draper looked interested.

"Oh, it all happened years ago, Sergeant. Seven or eight years ago, I would guess. Soon after we moved down here to Westbourne. Mark and Jack were ten or eleven then. They were great friends. Did everything together. It happened in the Easter holidays one year, as far as I remember. Mark had a collection of birds' eggs. He was crazy about them. You know what children can be like when they're into something like that. Well, the fact is, the two boys started to climb down the cliff one day – they were looking for seagulls' eggs. You know how the gulls build their nests in the cliff face. So, Mark was trying to get the eggs out of one of those nests – and he lost his footing and fell to his death … I expect you can imagine what it was like for Jack when that happened."

Nobody spoke for the next few moments.

"So you see," said Mrs Thomson at last, "after that, I don't think Jack would have wanted to go too near the edge of those cliffs."

Constable Briggs tried to continue. "Again, I'm afraid this may be painful for you. But we have to ask. Did your son have any enemies? People he didn't like? Or people who didn't like him? He was at sixth form college, you say. Was there ever any trouble with bullies? You know the kind of thing we mean."

Bruce Thomson understood. "You mean you think someone could have pushed him over the cliff? – No. No, I can't imagine it. Definitely not."

"When did you last see Jack?" asked Sergeant Draper.

"Yesterday evening," said Mary. "He went out at about half past six."

"Did he say where he was going?"

---

1 **Crawford** ['krɔ:fəd] • 8 **Easter** ['i:stə] Ostern, Oster- • 9 **collection** [kə'lekʃən] Sammlung • 14 **face** [feɪs] *hier:* Seite, Wand • 15 **to lose one's footing** [ˌlu:z wʌnz 'fʊtɪŋ] den Halt verlieren

"He just said he was meeting some friends. Here in Westbourne, I imagine. Now he's eighteen, he sometimes likes to meet his friends down at the pub. They usually go to the Red Lion in Victoria Street, I think. Jack never drinks much or anything. So we don't – we didn't mind."

"Were these close friends, then?" asked Constable Briggs.

"Well, I don't know. Just a few of the lads he played cricket with," said Bruce Thomson.

"He loved his cricket," added Mary.

"Hmm. Just one more question," said Sergeant Draper. "Did Jack have a girlfriend?"

"Oh yes. A very nice girl," said Mary. "Rebecca Harding. They were very close. They first met last September, I think. Jack was very fond of her, we know that."

"Maybe you can give us her address," said Sergeant Draper.

"Of course. She lives in Cornwall Road. Number 14, I think."

"Thanks, Mrs Thomson. Just one more thing we have to tell you both. I expect you know that in cases like this, there has to be a post-mortem. That means your son's body will be examined at the mortuary, and later – we don't know exactly when – there will be an inquest. The coroner has already been informed."

"An inquest?" asked Bruce Thomson. "I don't understand."

"The inquest, in cases like this, is the official inquiry – it's to establish the cause of death. It will be held at the coroner's court in Felton."

Mary Thomson's face had gone white.

"Here's my card," Constable Briggs told her. "It's got my phone number on it. So you can always contact me any

3 **pub** [pʌb] Kneipe, Wirtschaft • 4 **lion** ['laɪən] Löwe • 6 **close** [kləʊs] *hier:* eng (befreundet) • 13 **Rebecca Harding** [rɪˌbekə 'hɑ:dɪŋ] • 15 **to be fond of** [fɒnd əv] gerne mögen • 23 **mortuary** ['mɔ:tʃuəri] Leichenhalle • 29 **to establish** [ɪ'stæblɪʃ] festellen, klären • 31 **to go white** [gəʊ 'waɪt] blass werden

time – if there are any questions you want to ask, or if you need advice. I'll always be there to help you. OK?"

"Thank you, Constable."

"If I were you, I'd talk to your doctor tomorrow. Maybe he can recommend something to help you relax. Goodbye, Mrs Thomson. Mr Thomson."

"Oh, and we'll be back some time tomorrow to look at Jack's room," Sergeant Draper added. "It won't take us long. – It's OK, we can let ourselves out."

The two detectives left the house. Bruce and Mary Thomson stood at the window and watched them as they got into their car and drove away.

4 David Briggs at work

"Might be a good idea to go and see this Rebecca girl right away," said Sergeant Draper as they drove away from the Thomsons' house. "Cornwall Road is just round the corner."

"Isn't it a bit early, Steve? Can't it wait until tomorrow? She's the girlfriend – so the boy's death will be a shock for her ..."

"You're right. It's best to give her a bit of time. I tell you what. You go round to Cornwall Road on your own tomorrow afternoon and talk to Rebecca. While you're there, maybe I'll be able to contact the sixth form college. Ask a few questions. Maybe speak to one of Jack's teachers before they all go home. Then I'll pick you up and we'll go back to the Thomsons' place together."

"Right. So now what?"

"Back to the station, Dave. Plenty to do there. For a start, you can get to work on Jack's mobile – contact Cell Site Analysis. You know the routine. OK?"

• • •

15 round [raʊnd] um, herum • **28 station** [ˈsteɪʃn] Polizeirevier • **28 plenty** [ˈplenti] viel, eine Menge • **29 to get to work** [get‿tə ˈwɜːk] mit der Arbeit anfangen

David Briggs loved his job. He had always wanted to be a police officer. And it was great to be a detective, of course. But there was one thing he still found difficult, and that was something he quite often had to do. When there had been a death or an accident in the Westbourne area, he was often the person who had to tell the family the news. He had to go to the house and ring the doorbell. Had to talk to the people who were in shock.

Just like now. Here he was outside the door of 14, Cornwall Road. How would he manage it this time?

Mrs Harding came to the door. When she saw his card, her hand flew to her face. "Oh dear! I knew this would happen! Police! Oh well, come in, then. But don't get your hopes up too high! Rebecca's upstairs. She's in a terrible state! She's locked herself in her room. Been there all day. And all yesterday almost. I don't know what we're going to do about it. Maybe we'll have to get the doctor in ... Oh well, come upstairs, then. But I don't expect she'll open the door."

He did his best. "Hello, Rebecca," he called from outside her bedroom door. "My name's David Briggs. I'm a police constable. I'd just like to talk to you for a few moments. It won't take long. Can you open the door?"

There was no answer. "It'll be OK," he continued. "You needn't worry. Nobody wants to make trouble for you. We only want to help."

It took a long time, but in the end the door opened. Rebecca came out. Her face looked tired and pale, and her long brown hair was in an awful mess. She was wearing pyjamas. She looked at the young police officer, then looked away again. She said nothing.

Mrs Harding disappeared downstairs. "I'll just make some tea," she called. "You can sit down with her in the living room."

---

12 **Oh well.** [əʊ ˈwel] Na schön! • 14 **state** [steɪt] Zustand, Verfassung • 14 **to lock oneself in** [lɒk] sich einschließen • 27 **pale** [peɪl] blass • 29 **pyjamas** [pɪˈʒɑːməz] Schlafanzug

He went down and Rebecca followed. She chose a chair for herself that she could move near the window, and sat down. All the time he tried to talk to her, she continued to look straight out into the garden.

"Rebecca, I'm sorry I have to ask you these questions. But there are a few things we have to find out, OK? Now – when did you last see Jack?"

No reply. He tried again. "Did you meet him on Tuesday at all? After school, maybe?"

"No, I didn't meet him." Her voice was so quiet, he could hardly hear the words.

"When was the last time you spoke to him, then?"

She shrugged.

"So you're sure you didn't meet him on Tuesday evening?"

"Yes! – No! – I mean I didn't meet him, I mean I didn't talk to him … Oh, I don't know. Everything's so awful! I don't know anything any more. I can't – Oh, leave me alone! Just leave me alone! Please! I can't talk about it!" She began to cry. He noticed that she was shaking. Was she afraid to speak?

"It's OK to tell me about it," he said quietly. "Tell me where you were on Tuesday evening, Rebecca." Again, there was no reply.

In the end he decided to go. It was too early to talk to her yet, he could see that. "I have a feeling she might be more comfortable with a female officer," he said to Mrs Harding before he left. "I'll see what I can do. Oh, and there's something else we could try. Has she got any close friends who might know something – about her and Jack?"

"You could try Lauren Cox. Lauren's her best friend. Lives in Park Road. A new house at the end."

"Thanks for the tip, Mrs Harding. Goodbye."

• • •

13 **to shrug** [ʃrʌg] die Achseln zucken • 27 **to be comfortable** ['kʌmftəbl] sich wohl fühlen • 27 **female** ['fi:meɪl] weiblich • 31 **Lauren Cox** [ˌlɔ:rən 'kɒks]

He still had the chance to go to the house in Park Road before Sergeant Draper came to pick him up. There was plenty of time.

Lauren was alone at home. As soon as she realized he was a detective, she let the young constable in, and seemed very interested to talk to him.

"My mum's still at work. But that's OK. We can sit in the kitchen. – Is it about Jack Thomson? I heard what happened. Read about it too, of course. It was in all the newspapers today."

He explained why he had come.

"Yes, I expect it's the shock. No wonder she doesn't want to talk about it yet. – No, I haven't seen her at all since it happened. So, what exactly do you want to know?"

"Well, there are lots of questions I wanted to ask Rebecca, of course. But the most important one was about Tuesday evening – the evening when Jack died. Did she meet him that evening? Have you any idea, Lauren?"

"I'm quite sure she didn't meet him. That's definite."

"How can you be so sure?"

"Because they'd split up, that's why."

"Split up? How do you know?"

"Because she told me. Last weekend. We're best mates, right? She tells me everything. So, well, on Saturday she told me she'd definitely decided to split up with Jack."

"And have you seen her again since Saturday?"

"No, I haven't."

"Not even at school?"

"We go to different schools, so I don't see her every day. But I can tell you: When Rebecca Harding makes up her mind to do something, that's definite! They'd split up. It was all over. I expect she told him on Sunday."

13 since [sɪns] seit, seitdem • **32 over** ['əʊvə] vorbei • **32 to expect** [ɪk'spekt] *hier:* annehmen

5 Finding out more

“Split up, had they? Hmm. Well, if that’s true, maybe Jack really thought he had a reason to ride that motorbike up to the cliff top and end it all …” Sergeant Draper thought about it for a moment. “Who knows? It wouldn’t be the first time a teenager did a thing like that. If Rebecca was the love of his life – like his mother seems to think. Well …”

“Maybe Lauren was wrong?”

“Doesn’t sound like it, from what you’ve just told me, Dave. – OK, well, let’s look through everything here, then. We’ll start with his desk.”

They were in Jack’s bedroom. They were both surprised to see how tidy it was. Not at all like the teenagers’ bedrooms they usually saw! The bed was made, everything was in its place, there were no books, papers or clothes on the floor. Just a few school books on the desk, probably from Tuesday afternoon’s homework.

“Plenty of photos!” said Constable Briggs. “Rebecca wherever you look … Postcards, too! Here’s one from Spain.” He looked at the back. “Sure enough: ‘Love from Rebecca’. Hmm.”

Sergeant Draper was already looking in the drawers of the desk. “Papers. Pens. Pencil case. Batteries. An old watch. The usual stuff. There doesn’t seem to be a diary.”

“Boys don’t usually keep diaries, Steve.”

“You’re right. Oh well … Wait a minute. What’s this?” He took something out of the bottom drawer. It was a page from a newspaper. “At the back of the drawer, this was. I wonder why he kept it …”

“What’s the date on it, then?”

“30th of April. That was last week. – OK, let’s see. Any articles he could have been interested in? ‘South–West hit by stormy weather’? No … ‘Plans for new bridge at Tripton’?

---

20 sure enough [ˌʃʊərˌɪˈnʌf] Tatsächlich! • **22 drawer** [drɔː] Schublade • **24 usual** [ˈjuːʒl] üblich • **24 stuff** [stʌf] Zeug • **33 Tripton** [ˈtrɪptən]

No… But what about this, Dave? Listen: 'Felton punch–up victim dies in hospital.' This could be important."

They both read the short article.

'The 59–year–old man who was badly injured in a punch–up outside a pub in Felton in March died in Felton General Hospital yesterday. It was reported at the time that three youths were seen, but Felton Police have still not been able to trace them.'

"You think Jack could have been involved?" Constable Briggs wondered.

"No – he was hardly the type for that kind of thing, I'd say. Check it anyway, though, with Felton CID. Find out the details – where the punch–up was, and when exactly it happened, any details of the youths that were seen, etc."

"It's a wonder they weren't identified on CCTV."

1 **punch-up** ['pʌnʃʌp] Schlägerei • 2 **victim** ['vɪktɪm] Opfer • 8 **to trace s.o.** [treɪs] jdn aufspüren, ausfindig machen • 9 **to be involved (in s.th.)** [ɪn'vɒlvd] mit etwas zu tun haben • 12 **though** [ðəʊ] trotzdem, aber • 14 **youths** [ju:ðz] junge Männer • 15 **CCTV** ['si:si:ti:'vi:] Überwachungskamera

"That's true. Especially in a big town like Felton. – Well, Dave, we have to admit this article doesn't really seem to help much with our own case. It isn't marked at all. Maybe Jack never even read it! Let's see what's on the other side of the page ... Local sports news. Hey, this looks more like it: 'Cricket: St John's College First Eleven in fine form for new season.' And look! Jack Thomson's name is even mentioned. Chosen as the new Captain of their First Eleven."

"So it looks like we can forget about the punch-up in Felton, then!" said Constable Briggs.

"No, Dave. We can't forget about *anything* in our job, I'm afraid. It may be more important than you'd think."

"Only joking, Steve. I'll check, just like you said."

"Oh, and what about Jack's mobile? Have you got any details yet from Cell Site Analysis?"

"Yes, I've got the printout with me now. The details came in just before I left the station. Here you are."

"Thanks. – Well, there's certainly plenty of stuff here! We'll have to go through it all carefully. Have you looked at it yourself yet?"

"Haven't had time! I just noticed there are a lot of text messages from Rebecca. Hardly surprising, of course. – Oh, and there seems to be another girl Jack's been in contact with. Someone called Janice. Three or four messages from her. Things like 'Call me! Please!' and 'I still love you, Jack.'"

"Well, that's a surprise!" said Sergeant Draper. "Mrs Thomson knew nothing about *her,* I imagine! We'll have to find out who she is."

"Maybe Jack's cricket friends would know something about her and Jack."

"Maybe. We'll get their names from the Thomsons before we leave."

---

5 **local** [ˈləʊkəl] örtlich • 6 **the First Eleven** [fɜːst ɪˈlevn] die erste Mannschaft (cricket) • 17 **printout** [ˈprintaʊt] Ausdruck

"Oh, and there's a strange one here, look, Steve. 'Keep your mouth shut or else.' Sounds a bit suspicious to me!"

"You're right. Who's it from? Let me see the printout."

"I'm afraid it looks like it's from a top-up phone. Look, there's no phone number – only the name of the provider."

"That's bad. We probably won't be able to trace the sender of that one, then. It may be from a stolen mobile. Try, though. – Well, let's look at the date on it anyway. Here we are: It was sent on the first of May. Interesting. Just one day after the date of the newspaper we were looking at. – Oh, and Dave, remember to get details of Jack's own messages, too. That's important."

"OK. – And look at the last text message he got, Steve. The last of all. The day he died. It just says: 'OK. CU 2nite.'"

"Who's it from?"

"Wait a minute … Let's check the number … What? It's from Rebecca's mobile! But they'd split up! At least, that's what the Cox girl said!"

"Well, maybe she was wrong after all …"

6 At the Red Lion

Tom Barker looked round the bar of the Red Lion and smiled to himself. Yes, Clare had been right to suggest they should take the Red Lion. It had been a risk, of course. They'd never had a pub before. But they'd decided to take the chance. Nice little pub it was, just in the centre of Westbourne. Quite near the beach, too, couldn't be better. And the tourist season was just starting, that was the great thing about a seaside town. Visitors to the town meant customers. Yes, he and the wife were doing well. And it was only their second year!

1 **Keep your mouth shut!** [ki:p jə 'maʊθ ˌʃʌt] Halt die Klappe! • 6 **provider** [prə'vaɪdə] *hier:* Telefongesellschaft • 8 **sender** ['sendə] Absender • 20 **after all** [a:ftər‿'ɔ:l] doch • 21 **bar** [bɑ:] Bar, Theke • 22 **Clare** [kleə]

"Hello, Tom. Busy again this evening, I see!" It was Steve Draper. The detective. Tom guessed he must be on a new case. So far, whenever Steve had come into the pub, he'd had some kind of questions to ask.

"Hello, Steve. Good to see you. Everything OK?"

"Fine, Tom. – I'll have a pint of bitter, please."

"Right you are. Nice evening again. But it looks like the good weather may be over by tomorrow. Rain's on the way, they say."

"Maybe so. – Tom, have you got a few moments? There are one or two things I was wanting to ask you, if you aren't too busy just now."

"That's OK, Steve. Is it about the Thomson boy? Terrible tragedy, terrible. Such a nice lad. Clare heard about it before I did, actually ..."

"Yes, I'm afraid that's the case I'm working on just now. The boy's parents thought he was probably down here on Tuesday evening. Just a short time before it happened, that would be."

"That's right. He came in at around 6.45, I think, and must have been here for half an hour or an hour. Had a couple of pints with his mates. Nice lads, all of them."

"You know them all, then?"

"Well, not really. But they seem to be good lads. Always polite. Never make any trouble."

"So you don't remember exactly when they left?"

"Well, no, but I remember the others left without Jack. He stayed here – still had some beer left in his glass. He wasn't on his own for long, though. Two other lads came in and sat down at his table – it was the one over there in the corner. Jack seemed to know them, I noticed, but I must say, I'd never seen them in here with him before. I had the feeling right away that there was going to be trouble, don't ask me why. And sure enough, there was!"

3 **whenever** [wen'evə] jedes Mal wenn • 6 **pint** [paɪnt] ‚eine Halbe' • 6 **bitter** ['bɪtə] Bitter (dunkles Bier) • 7 **Right you are!** [ˌraɪt ju 'ɑː] In Ordnung! • 21 **a couple of** ['kʌpl əv] ein, zwei

Steve looked at the landlord closely. "What kind of trouble?"

Tom Barker shrugged. "It was busy, so I couldn't hear what they were saying. But I could see they were having an argument about something. Not nice at all, I'm afraid."

"Did it get violent?"

"No, I wouldn't say that. Jack left before it got out of control. He was a quiet lad normally – not a trouble maker."

"And the two boys?"

"Ooh, let me see. They left a minute or so later, I would say."

"Well, thanks for the information, Tom. Do you know these boys' names? Where they live?"

"Afraid not. We've seen them in here a few times, but I don't think they live anywhere in Westbourne. Sorry, I can't help you there. – Wait, I'll just ask Clare."

His wife was at the other end of the bar. She remembered the two boys, but had no idea who they were. "I didn't see them when they were in here with the Thomson boy," she told Sergeant Draper. "I was helping chef in the kitchen. But later on, when Tom was serving in the other bar at the back, I was in here myself for the rest of the evening. And – at around 8.30 or nine o'clock, I think it was – those boys came in here again and got drunk! You wouldn't believe it! Blind drunk! One of the customers took them outside in the end, it had got so bad."

"You didn't tell me about that, Clare!" said Tom.

"Well, no, you were busy just then – and later I didn't think about it." She turned to Sergeant Draper. "It happens all the time, of course. Nothing unusual when lads get drunk. Girls, too, sometimes. But I needn't tell you that, Steve. What you see in *your* job is a lot worse, I'm sure!"

---

1 landlord ['lænlɔːd] Wirt • **7 out of control** [ˌaʊt əv kən'trəʊl] außer Kontrolle • **8 trouble maker** ['trʌblmeɪkə] Unruhestifter • **21 chef** [ʃef] der Küchenchef, Koch, Köchin • **22 to serve** [sɜːv] bedienen • **25 to get drunk** [get 'drʌŋk] sich betrinken • **26 blind drunk** [blaɪnd 'drʌŋk] stockbetrunken

It was true. Sergeant Draper thought of Jack's body on the beach, and how he had felt when he arrived at the scene that Wednesday morning. Only yesterday! It seemed much longer ago. "Pity you can't give me any names," he said.

"No – but there's one thing that might help," said Tom. "Those two were in here last Friday, as far as I remember. Maybe they'll come in again tomorrow. Can't be sure, of course. But they might."

"Thanks for the tip, then, Tom. I'll try it. See you again tomorrow. Good night!"

7 That's what friends are for

Would Lauren never be able to get Rebecca out of the house?

"Come on, Becky! This isn't going to kill you, you know," she said to her friend. "We're only going to the Milkmaid Café. It'll do you good to go out. You can't sit around at home for ever."

"I know, Lauren. It's just that ... Oh, everything is so awful! You can't imagine how I feel."

"Yes, I can! I know it's difficult for you. I understand that. But you'll go crazy if you stay on your own all day and never go out. – It's OK, I've got an umbrella. Come on!"

• • •

Ten minutes later, the two girls were sitting at their favourite table in the Milkmaid Café. Lauren ordered two mugs of Latte. She looked at Rebecca. What was wrong with her? Every time someone came into the café, she looked away or looked down at the floor. Lauren noticed that she had started to bite her fingernails. That was definitely

4 **longer ago** [ˌlɒŋgər‿əˈgəʊ] länger her • 15 **milkmaid** [ˈmɪlkmeɪd] Milchmädchen • 22 **umbrella** [ʌmˈbrelə] Regenschirm • 25 **Latte** [ˈlæteɪ] Milchkaffee • 28 **to bite one's fingernails** [ˌbeɪt wʌnz ˈfɪŋgəneɪlz] an seinen Fingernägeln kauen

something she had never done before! The tablets the doctor had prescribed to make her calmer didn't seem to be much help, Lauren thought. Anyway, next week she would probably have to go back to school. Maybe by then she would feel a bit better. Lauren hoped so.

The hot drink seemed to do Rebecca good. Would she start to talk now? She looked out of the window and stared at the sea, sad and grey now that the weather had changed. Lauren waited.

"I feel guilty, Lauren," Rebecca said at last, very slowly. "So, so guilty!"

"But why? You haven't done anything wrong! What happened to Jack wasn't … Well, it wasn't your fault. Not really." She looked away.

"Oh, Lauren! Stop it! I know I told you I wanted to split up with Jack. You remember what I said?"

"Of course. It was only a few days ago. I remember it OK. Everything you told me."

"Well … That was how I felt then. Of course it was. It was all true! But now … Oh, Lauren, I feel so different about it now! Now that Jack is … gone …, I've suddenly realized how much he meant to me! I love him, Lauren!"

Rebecca put her head in her hands. Lauren saw that she was crying again.

"I can understand you feel like that now, Becky. Jack meant a lot to you, I know that. And *you* meant everything to him! So – why did you want to split up with him? When you told me on Saturday, I couldn't believe it!"

Rebecca started to bite her fingernails again. "It's hard to explain."

Lauren wanted to know. "Tell me, Becky, come on! That's what friends are for!"

"I know, Lauren."

"Well, then?"

---

2 to prescribe [prɪˈskraɪb] verschreiben • **10 guilty** [ˈgɪlti] schuldig • **13 It wasn't your fault.** [ɪt ˌwɒznt ˈjɔː ˈfɔːlt] Es war nicht deine Schuld.

"I can't explain … Things just weren't going well. Jack's life was a complete mess. I couldn't deal with it any more. All his problems …"

"What problems, Becky? At college or what? I thought he was doing so well."

"He was! – They were more like – er – personal problems. You know?"

"Personal problems? What do you mean? Did you think he might have found someone else?"

"Oh, Lauren! You've no idea …"

Rebecca turned her face away from Lauren and looked out of the window again. The rain was coming down heavily now, a strong wind had got up, and a long line of white waves was crashing onto the beach. "You see, it started a few weeks ago … There was this boy … And …"

"A boy?" Lauren sat up straight in her chair. "A boy?? Rebecca, you surprise me! So there was a *boy* in all this? – Wow! Where did you meet him, then?"

"Stop it, Lauren!" Rebecca sounded angry. "You've no idea what you're talking about! You're so stupid! Sometimes I really hate you! I wish I hadn't told you anything now!"

"OK, OK, I'm sorry. – Let's be friends again. Come on!"

But Rebecca had started to cry again. Lauren put her hand on her friend's arm, but Rebecca pushed it away. "Leave me alone."

Lauren ordered two more mugs of Latte. After a few moments, she tried to get Rebecca to talk to her again. "I'm so curious, though, Becky. How did Jack react when you told him you wanted to split up?"

Rebecca looked at her and shook her head. "You've got it all wrong, Lauren. I wanted to … But I never actually told him – in the end … It all worked out differently."

---

13 **to get up** [get‿'ʌp] aufkommen • 14 **onto** ['ɒntə] auf • 16 **to sit up straight** [sɪt‿ʌp 'streɪt] sich aufrichten • 20 **stupid** ['stju:pɪd] dumm, blöd • 28 **to react** [ri'ækt] reagieren • 30 **You've got it all wrong.** [ju:v ˌgɒt ɪt ɔ:l 'rɒŋ] Du kapierst es nicht. • 32 **to work out differently** [wɜ:k aʊt 'dɪfrntli] anders laufen

"What?! But you – "

"Quiet, Lauren! Look who's coming."

It was Samantha Brown, a girl they knew from the tennis club. She had come into the café and seen the two girls. Now she was coming up to their table.

"Oh, Becky, I'm so sorry!" she said. "I just can't believe this about Jack! With all your problems anyway – and now this! Oh, it must be especially horrible for you now …"

"*My* problems? What do you mean?" But when Rebecca looked at Lauren, she suddenly understood what Samantha was talking about. Lauren turned away guiltily when she saw the look of horror on her friend's face.

"Lauren! Can you never keep anything to yourself?" Rebecca got up from the table and ran out of the café.

8 A suspicious alibi

When Steven Draper and David Briggs came into the Red Lion together on Friday evening, they went straight up to the bar. Tom Barker saw them at once and came over.

"Hello, Steve. Hi, Dave. You're in luck. I thought you might be. Those two young blokes we were talking about yesterday – well, you'll be interested to know they're here again now." He raised his eyebrows. "Over there. The tall one with the dark hair, and the redhead with the grey sweatshirt. See?"

"Thanks," said Sergeant Draper. "Come on, then, Dave."

"Wait a moment, Steve. Correct me if I'm wrong – but the one with the dark hair, I think we know him from somewhere. I can't remember the case exactly, but I could swear he's got a criminal record."

"You may be right. We'll look him up on the data base. OK, so let's go and have a little talk with them."

The detectives went over to the two boys and showed their CID cards. Without a moment's delay, Sergeant Draper began: "We've got a few questions for you two, OK?" He took a photo of Jack Thomson out of his pocket and showed it to them. "Do you know this boy at all?" he asked.

Constable Briggs watched them closely. The smaller of the two boys looked at the photo quickly, then turned his face away. The other, taller boy looked straight at Sergeant Draper and said, "No. Why? What's all this about, then?"

"So you're sure you've never seen this boy before?" said Constable Briggs. He looked from one boy to the other. Their faces looked blank, but at the same time they both seemed nervous. He noticed that the smaller boy with

5 **bloke** [bləʊk] Typ, Kerl • 7 **to raise one's eyebrows** [ˌreɪz wʌnz ˈaibraʊz] die Augenbrauen hochziehen • 8 **redhead** [ˈredhed] Rothaarige(r) • 15 **to swear** [sweə] schwören • 15 **to have a criminal record** [ˌkrɪmɪnl ˈrekɔ:d] vorbestraft sein • 16 **data base** [ˈdeɪtəˌbeɪs] Datenbank • 30 **blank** [blæŋk] ausdruckslos

the red hair had a nervous tic at the corner of his left eye. "Think carefully, now."

There was no answer.

"It seems to me you two guys have bad memories," said Sergeant Draper. "Very bad. But I think we can get you to remember! You may not realize this, but we already know that you were both in here on Tuesday evening – together with Jack Thomson, the boy in this photo. We also know that there was an argument between the three of you. So don't try any more lies! You were seen in this pub here, and you know it!"

Again, the boys gave no answer. The boy with the red hair shrugged his shoulders.

"Right," said Constable Briggs. "Just in case you didn't know this – Jack Thomson, the boy in the photo, was found dead on Westbourne beach on Wednesday morning. – Now, what were you two doing on Tuesday evening between 7.30 and nine o'clock? Come on. Where were you?" He looked at the redhead closely. "Well?"

"At the cinema. We were in Felton. We went to see a film." The tic at the corner of his eye was getting worse now.

"Oh yes?" said Sergeant Draper. "So you left here at 7.30 and went to the cinema in Felton, right? By bus? Fifteen miles by bus? Then watched a film – and got back here again in time to get drunk in this pub by 9.30? You think we're going to believe that story?"

"We didn't go by bus! We've got motorbikes. We ..."

"Motorbikes, eh? Well, that's interesting!"

"What film did you see, then?" asked Constable Briggs. "We're listening."

"What's that got to do with you?" said the taller boy rudely.

"I expect they've forgotten, Dave!" said Sergeant Draper. He looked at the other detective and raised his eyebrows.

1 **tic** [tɪk] (nervöses) Zucken • 4 **memory** ['meməri] Gedächtnis • 14 **just in case** [dʒəst ɪn 'keɪs] für den Fall, dass • 25 **in time** [ɪn 'taɪm] rechtzeitig

Then he turned to the boys again. "OK, you two. Enough of this rubbish. We're taking you down to the station for questioning."

9 Questions – and more questions

"Name and address?" Constable Briggs asked the taller of the two boys.

"Jason Oldfield. 61, Brook Road, Woodbridge."

"Age?"

"Nineteen."

"And you?" He looked at the boy with the red hair.

"Kevin Long. 53, Queen's Drive, Woodbridge. I'm eighteen."

"OK, Dave, you can leave it to me now," said Sergeant Draper. "I'll deal with the two of them while you get what we need from the data base." Constable Briggs left the room.

Sergeant Draper looked from one of the boys to the other. "Well, here we are, then. Ready? Before we start, I must warn you: You don't have to say anything. But there will be an inquest in a few weeks. At the coroner's court in Felton. About Jack Thomson's death. You two may have to appear in court, you realize that? So, if you don't mention something now that comes out later in court, it may be harmful for you. Anything you say now may be given in evidence. Is that clear?"

The boys looked blank. Sergeant Draper wondered whether they had understood.

"OK, then. Now. Think carefully. I'm asking you both. Were you up at the top of the cliffs above Westbourne beach on Tuesday evening at all?"

---

2 **for questioning** [fə ˈkwestʃən,ɪŋ] zwecks Verhör • 6 **Jason Oldfield** [ˌdʒeɪsn ˈəʊldfi:ld] • 12 **You can leave it to me.** [ju: kən ˌli:v ɪt tə ˈmi:] Du kannst es mir überlassen. • 21 **to appear** [əˈpɪə] erscheinen • 23 **harmful** [ˈhɑ:mfəl] *hier:* belastend • 23 **in evidence** [ɪn ˈevidəns] als Beweismaterial

The boys said nothing. Kevin looked quickly at Jason, then looked away again. The detective continued quietly. "Well, I'm waiting for an answer. Were you up on those cliffs at all?" He stared long and hard into Kevin's face. At last Kevin spoke.

"We told you. We were at the cinema. We –"

"Come on, now, Kevin. You know that's not true." He looked at the other boy. "Well, Jason? What do you say about it? No more lies, now. It doesn't look good, you know."

Jason looked down at the floor. He said nothing.

"It's OK," said Sergeant Draper. "Take your time, both of you. I can wait. You can stay here at the station all night if necessary."

He took out a packet of cigarettes and put it down quietly on the desk in front of him. "Do you smoke?" he asked.

"Oh, thanks!" Kevin said and stretched out his hand.

But Sergeant Draper laughed, and put the packet back in his pocket. "Surely you didn't think I was offering you a cigarette?" he said. "Oh, no. It was just a general question, that's all! And you answered it nicely."

The boys looked at each other. Sergeant Draper could see that they were getting nervous again.

"OK, no more trick questions, then. From now on, it's serious. Dead serious. Now, both of you, listen carefully. A couple of cigarette ends were found at the top of those cliffs. Found by our Scene Of Crime Officers on Wednesday morning. *Fresh* cigarette ends, you understand?"

"So what?" said Jason. He sounded aggressive suddenly. "Are we the only people around here that smoke?"

When he saw that Jason was talking again, Kevin sat up straighter and joined in. "You can't prove those fags were ours!" he shouted. "What do you know? Nothing!"

---

14 necessary ['nesəsri] nötig • **15 packet** ['pækɪt] Schachtel • **17 to stretch out** [stretʃ 'aʊt] ausstrecken • **20 general** ['dʒenrəl] allgemein • **25 serious** ['sɪərɪəs] ernst • **30 around here** [əˌraʊnd 'hɪə] hier in der Gegend • **32 to join in** [dʒɔɪn 'ɪn] mitmachen • **32 to prove** [pruːv] beweisen • **32 fag** [fæg] Kippe

"Don't be so sure," said Sergeant Draper quietly. "Have you two never heard of fingerprints? Or DNA testing?"

At that moment, Constable Briggs came back in. "Got this from the data base," he said, and gave the other detective a printout. Then he sat down and waited.

"Thanks, Dave." There was silence in the room while the sergeant read everything through.

"Well," he said at last. "This printout here gives us a lot of information about you, Jason. Just in case you've forgotten, I'll explain. Jason Oldfield, you have a criminal record. In November last year, you were in court. You were charged with assault and criminal damage. You were found guilty – and you were given a year's community order."

Jason said nothing.

"Now, Jason," the sergeant continued, "you know exactly what that means! You got the community order last November. Six months ago. OK so far? Now, a year's

6 **silence** ['saɪləns] Stille • 12 **assault** [ə'sɔ:lt] Körperverletzung, Überfall • 12 **criminal damage** [ˌkrɪmɪnl 'dæmɪdʒ] Sachschaden durch Gewalteinwirkung • 13 **community order** [kəˌmjunətɪ 'ɔ:də] Verurteilung zu gemeinnütziger Arbeit

community order means that you have to behave well – really well, Jason – for a whole year! No more trouble with the police for a whole year! And that year won't end until *next* November, Jason. I'm sure you realize what it could mean if you're involved in another crime before the end of that year. Do you realize, Jason?"

Again there was no reply.

"It could mean prison, Jason. If the crime was serious enough. Murder, for example … Or manslaughter …"

Kevin, the younger boy, suddenly broke down. He began to cry. "We didn't kill Jack Thomson, we didn't!" he called out in a strange, high voice. "You've got to believe me! We didn't kill him! It wasn't like that – it wasn't like that at all!"

While Kevin was crying out, a mobile phone began to ring. Jason put a hand in his pocket. Constable Briggs stopped him. "I'll take that mobile if you don't mind, Jason," he said. "We need to check a few things."

"What? You can't take my mobile! It'll be my mum – she'll want to know why I'm not back yet! Let me –"

"You'll get the phone back tomorrow," said Sergeant Draper. "Use this one here if you want to contact your mother. – You both live in Woodbridge, right? Tell her you'll be brought back home in half an hour – in a police car."

• • •

When he went to bed later that evening, Sergeant Draper was still thinking about the case. Some things seemed clear – but there were still questions he found difficult to answer. What exactly had happened on that Tuesday evening? He tried to imagine it all …

Jack Thomson had been at the Red Lion with friends. Harmless enough, it seemed. Later, Jason Oldfield and Kevin Long had come in. They knew Jack. Had they gone to the Red Lion deliberately, to meet him? If so, why? How did they know him, anyway? And what was the argument

---

5 **crime** [kraɪm] Verbrechen • 9 **murder** ['mɜːdə] Mord • 9 **manslaughter** ['mænˌslɔːtə] Totschlag • 10 **to break down** [breɪk 'daʊn] *hier:* zusammenbrechen • 11 **to call out** [kɔːl‿'aʊt] aufschreien • 30 **harmless** ['hɑːmləs] harmlos

about? Clearly, Jason and Kevin were in no hurry to tell the police their secret. What were they hiding? They certainly seemed aggressive – and violent. Sergeant Draper thought again about the newspaper article they had found in Jack's bedroom. About the punch-up in Felton back in March and the death of the man in hospital. Could this have anything to do with the case? The CID in Felton had not been able to solve that crime. But three youths were mentioned. Was it possible that Jack and these two other boys had been involved? After all, Jason Oldfield had already been found guilty of assault before. Why not again?

The detective turned his thoughts to the scene on the cliff top. Why had Jack gone up there? Had he planned to meet someone there? If so, who? Rebecca? It seemed probable. That last text message – 'CU 2nite' – had been from her. But on the other hand, the meeting place itself hadn't actually been mentioned ... So far, Rebecca had told the police nothing at all. The only thing she had been definite about was that she had *not* met Jack that evening ... Or was she lying? And what about Janice? The other girl who had left messages on Jack's mobile? Had he planned to meet *her* that evening? Could she be the reason why Jack had behaved so strangely over the last few weeks? Maybe – when they discovered her identity, tomorrow he hoped – she might be able to explain a few things.

Jason and Kevin had not exactly admitted that they had been up at the cliff top. But from the way they had reacted when he mentioned the cigarette ends, he felt sure they were theirs. If so, it would be easy to prove. On the other hand, the cigarette ends themselves proved nothing. Even if the two boys had followed Jack after he left the Red Lion, even if they had actually been with him at the cliff top, there was nothing to prove they had pushed him over the edge. All the police had so far was circumstantial evidence.

---

8 **to solve** [sɒlv] lösen • 12 **thought** [θɔ:t] Gedanke • 29 **on the other hand** [ɒn ði 'ʌðə ˌhænd] andererseits • 34 **circumstantial evidence** [sɜ:kəmˌstænʃl 'evɪdns] Indizienbeweis

Unless one – or both – of the boys made a confession, the evidence they had was clearly not enough. Steven Draper knew they were not allowed to try to get the boys to make a confession, for example through undue pressure. A confession that was made under pressure would not be valid in court.

The coroner had already agreed to delay the inquest until a later date, so the police would have time to collect more evidence. Steven Draper hoped the next few days would help them to discover what they needed to know.

He tried to sort out some of the details of the case in his head. But he found it hard to think clearly now. It was a long time before he finally fell asleep.

10 The inquest

When Rebecca woke up that Thursday morning, she knew at once it had come – the day she had dreaded so much. She had that odd feeling in her stomach again. It was a feeling she had often had recently. Now it was especially bad.

It was still too early to get up. Her thoughts turned – like they always did – to Jack. And to how all the trouble had started. When was it? It must have been in March. Yes. That was when she had first noticed something was wrong. He never seemed to listen when she was talking to him. He didn't even seem interested in her any more! At first she had wondered if he had met someone else. Or was it that Janice girl, the one he had gone out with a few times last summer? Rebecca knew Janice still liked Jack. Janice was certainly jealous of *her*, anybody could see that! So

1 **unless** [ənˈles] außer wenn • 4 **undue pressure** [ˌʌndjuː ˈpreʃə] Nötigung • 5 **pressure** [ˈpreʃə] Druck, Zwang • 6 **valid** [ˈvælɪd] gültig • 7 **to delay** [dɪˈleɪ] verschieben • 15 **to dread sth.** [dred] sich vor etwas fürchten • 22 **to be wrong** [rɒŋ] los sein

she'd had a little talk with Jack, but he had made it quite clear that Janice didn't mean anything to him any more. In fact, he hated it when Janice tried to get back into his life. Rebecca believed him.

But the situation was driving her crazy. She asked Jack again and again what was wrong. In the end, one afternoon when they were walking on the beach, alone together, he told her. She couldn't believe it at first, it was so horrible! It had happened in Felton, one Saturday evening. Jack told her he had come out of the cinema and was walking through a dark street on his way back to the car park where he had left his motorbike. Suddenly, some people came out of a small pub – a man and two lads. The man was drunk, and was provoking them – and intimidating them. It was a shock for Jack when he recognized one of the lads – someone he knew from his old school. Before Jack realized what was happening, the situation got out of control. The man started to attack the boys. Then the one that Jack knew hit the man, hard, so he fell on to the street. After that, he and the other boy kicked the man a few times until he fell with a crash, headfirst, down the steps to a public toilet.

It was then that the boys saw Jack. They suddenly realized that they had been watched. Before Jack knew what was happening, the boy he had recognized started to shout at him like a maniac. "You saw nothing, OK? Nothing, you understand?" He looked at Jack's face in the light of a street lamp. Jack's heart sank when he realized the boy recognized him. "So leave the police out of this! You hear me? If you go to the police, I'll kill you!"

When she heard the story, Rebecca had at once understood Jack's feelings. He had been too scared to go to the police. But on the other hand, he felt guilty because

---

2 **in fact** [ɪn ˈfækt] in Wirklichkeit • 14 **to provoke** [prəˈvəʊk] provozieren • 14 **to intimidate** [ɪnˈtɪmɪdeɪt] einschüchtern • 15 **to recognize** [ˈrekəgnaɪz] erkennen • 21 **headfirst** [hed ˈfɜːst] mit dem Kopf vorraus • 28 **street lamp** [ˈstriːt læmp] Straßenlaterne • 29 **out of this** [ˈaʊt‿əv ˌðɪs] aus dem Spiel

he was hiding information that the police needed to have. And the worst part was this. The boy knew who Jack was, so if Jack reported what he had seen to the police, the boy would know who had given him away – and would easily be able to find Jack …

"Rebecca! Are you coming?" It was her mother's voice. In a flash, Rebecca was back in her bedroom at home. On the day of the inquest. It was time to go downstairs for breakfast.

• • •

Quarter past ten. Rebecca sat at the back of the car. Her mother was driving, and her father was trying to find his favourite station on the radio. It was only a fifteen-mile journey to Felton. The inquest would start at eleven.

Rebecca looked out of the window, but she didn't notice the beautiful landscape outside. Again, she was lost in her own thoughts. Her parents didn't try to get her to talk. They

4 **to give s.o. away** [gɪv ˌsʌmwʌn əˈweɪ] jdn verraten • 7 **in a flash** [ɪn ə ˈflæʃ] in Sekundenschnelle • 10 **at the back** [ət ðə ˈbæk əv] hinten

had already tried so often, but always without success. They felt sorry for her – but what could they do?

Rebecca's thoughts had gone back to that day at the end of April. The day when Jack had seen that article in the local newspaper. The man that those boys had beaten up in Felton had died of his injuries! After that, things got worse than ever. Jack's guilty feelings left him no peace. They got so bad that he couldn't talk to her about anything else. She began to wish he had never told her about it all. The terrible secret was more than she could stand. In the end, she had made the decision. She wanted to split up with Jack...

• • •

They arrived at the coroner's court early. Rebecca and her parents were taken to their seats near Mr and Mrs Thomson. Mr Thomson sat there very straight and correct. His wife looked paler and thinner than Rebecca remembered. The detectives in charge of the case had not come into the court yet.

Rebecca felt tense and worried. Her mother had told her to relax, but how could she? The thought of what she knew seemed like a heavy weight on her shoulders. She tried not to think of it all, but the events of that day – Jack's last day! – started to appear in front of her eyes like a film that she couldn't switch off.

• • •

Yes, she had arranged to meet Jack at their favourite place – the little seat near the cliff top with the sea view they both loved so much. She was planning to tell Jack it was all over, that everything had got too much for her. It would be difficult, but she felt she had made the right decision ...

She looked at her watch as she walked up the cliff path. It was just after eight. She was a few minutes late. As she got

---

5 **to beat up** [biːt ˈʌp] zusammenschlagen • 7 **peace** [piːs] Ruhe, Frieden • 19 **tense** [tens] angespannt • 21 **weight** [weɪt] Gewicht • 24 **to switch off** [swɪtʃ ˈɒf] auschalten • 25 **to arrange** [əˈreɪndʒ] vereinbaren

nearer the top, she suddenly heard voices. Angry voices! Jack's voice was one of them. What was going on? Had he brought someone with him? She hoped not! She left the cliff path and walked past a group of bushes. Then she saw them. Jack and two boys she didn't know. Near the top of the cliff, their outline against the evening sky. They were in the middle of a terrible argument. Suddenly one of the boys tried to hit Jack, but he managed to duck out of the way. That's when she started to feel really scared. These must be the boys from the punch–up in Felton. They must be! Rebecca stood there, too afraid to move. She was glad they hadn't seen her.

Then everything happened very quickly. As the argument got more violent, Jack and the two other boys somehow moved nearer the edge of the cliff. The taller of the two boys hit Jack in the stomach, and he fell over. When he tried to get up again, he stumbled – and fell into a bush that was growing at the cliff edge. Part of the bush broke away under Jack's weight, and he fell off the cliff. It was all over in a few seconds.

Rebecca screamed in horror. She couldn't stop. She screamed and screamed. She didn't care if they saw her now. A moment later, she realized they were pushing Jack's motorbike to the top of the cliff. Then, together, the two boys threw it over the edge in desperation.

She suddenly felt the danger she was in. But when she tried to run away from them, the two boys chased after her and stopped her. The taller boy shook her arm and shouted at her, and she never forgot his words. "If you tell anyone about this, we'll kill you!"

• • •

Eleven o'clock. Rebecca couldn't believe her eyes. She had expected the inquest would be just a small thing. But no! It almost looked like one of those court scenes from a

---

7 in the middle of [ɪn ðə 'mɪdl ʌv] mitten in • **8 to duck** [dʌk] ausweichen, sich ducken • **14 somehow** ['sʌmhaʊ] irgendwie • **17 to stumble** ['stʌmbl] stolpern • **25 desperation** [ˌdespə'reɪʃn] Verzweiflung

film. There was even a witness box, and a jury–box! When the members of the jury came in and sat down in the jury box, she hardly dared to look at them. In fact, she tried not to look at anyone at all. The two detectives, Sergeant Draper and Constable Briggs, had just arrived. And – to Rebecca's horror – the two boys from the cliff–top scene were in the court now, too. When she saw them, her heart began to beat so hard, she thought it might burst. Before she had time to think, the coroner opened the inquest.

"I call upon Mr Bruce Thomson to give evidence."

Jack's father had to explain – on oath, even – how he had identified Jack's body. It didn't take long.

"Thank you, Mr Thomson. You can stand down. – I now call upon Mr Robert Williams to give evidence."

Mr Williams was the forensic pathologist who had been in charge of the post-mortem. Rebecca's stomach began to feel bad again. She tried not to listen to what he was

3 **to dare** [deə] sich trauen • 8 **to beat** [bi:t] schlagen • 8 **to burst** [bɜ:st] platzen • 10 **to call upon** [kɔ:l ə'pɒn] in den Zeugenstand rufen • 12 **to identify** [aɪ'dentifaɪ] identifizieren • 13 **to stand down** [stænd 'daʊn] den Zeugenstand verlassen

saying. By now, her thoughts – and her whole body – were in a turmoil. She had never in her whole life felt so scared as she felt now. Those two boys – the tall one with the dark hair that had hit Jack, and the smaller one, the redhead – were looking at her, she could feel it!

How much did the police know? Had the boys made a confession? She suddenly realized something – and her heart sank. If they had not made a confession, it meant that she, Rebecca, was the only person in the whole world that knew the truth … Another thought was going round her head at the same time. She knew some people had heard that she had split up with Jack. If the coroner's verdict was suicide, everyone would at once think that she was to blame …

"Well, Mr Williams," the coroner was saying. "In your opinion, could Jack Thomson's death be a case of suicide?"

"I would say," Mr Williams replied slowly, "it is possible, yes. But that doesn't mean it is probable."

"Thank you, Mr Williams. You can stand down. – I now call upon Rebecca Harding to give evidence."

Rebecca gasped. It couldn't be! Surely, the two boys would have to give evidence first?

"Rebecca Harding, please."

"But – But can't I – er – can't I be asked later? I – "

"I'm sorry, Miss Harding. The court would like to hear your evidence *now,* please. And remember – all evidence in this court is taken on oath."

Rebecca was shaking now. Out of the corner of her eye, she could see that the two boys from the cliff top scene were looking at her. What would they do to her if she dared to tell the court now what she had seen? In a flash, the tall boy's awful words came back to her: "…we'll kill you!" Would they? … But if she kept the terrible secret to herself,

2 turmoil ['tɜːmɔɪl] Tumult, Durcheinander • **10 truth** [truːθ] Wahrheit • **14 to be to blame** [bleɪm] an etw schuld sein

how would she feel then? Could she live with herself if she knew she had not told the whole truth in court? Wouldn't her guilty feelings be even worse than Jack's had been?

She was trapped. The pressure was greater than anything she had ever known ... But surely, she tried to convince herself, surely her evidence would be enough to put those boys in prison. Or would it? And, even if it was, what would happen when they came out?

Suddenly she realized that the coroner was speaking again. "Rebecca Harding, please. The court is waiting to hear your evidence, Miss Harding."

As she left her seat, a female officer took her arm. A moment later, Rebecca was in the witness box.

Everyone in the court was looking at her. She took a deep breath and closed her eyes for a moment. There was a tense silence before the coroner began his questions.

15 **to take a deep breath** [teɪk ə ˌdiːp ˈbreθ] tief Luft holen

Exercises

1 On the cliffs

Later that day, Eve sends one of her friends an e-mail – with news of what happened when she went out with her dog. What does she write?

2 Detectives on the scene

Find the right facts. Then put the correct words in the grid.

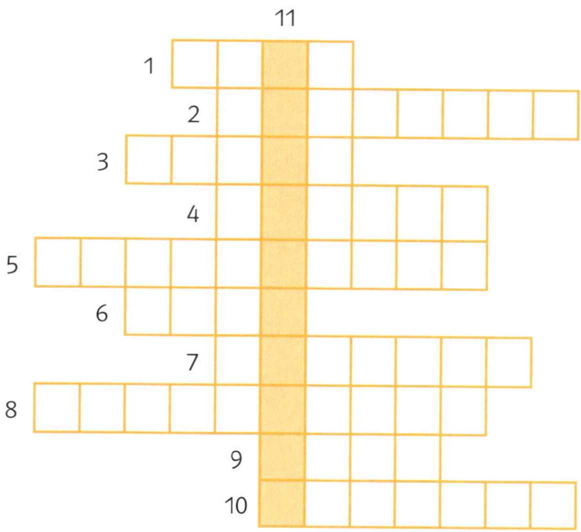

After the area around the (1) had been closed, the CID had to be called. (2) Draper first thought it might be (10) – not an accident – because the boy wasn't wearing a (4). Constable Briggs agreed this was (5). The time of (3) was between 8 and 9 pm. Fresh cigarette (9) and other clues were found at the top of the cliffs. A mobile was (8) on a (6) behind some bushes. Soon an 18-year-old boy was reported (7) by his parents. – Did you know? CID (11) don't wear uniform.

3 First inquiries

Explain what the detectives find out about …
a) how Jack behaved recently; b) his schoolwork;
c) Jack and Mark Crawford; d) Jack's friends and free time activities

4 David Briggs at work

1. *How does David Briggs feel about his work as a police officer? Think about the job. Would YOU enjoy it? First think of the positive sides. Then imagine: what might be difficult – or dangerous?*
2. *What questions would YOU like to ask Rebecca?*

5 Finding out more

1. *Tick (✓) the correct facts. (More than one could be right!)*
   a) In Jack's bedroom: The police find ☐ photos of Rebecca; ☐ a diary; ☐ books on the floor; ☐ a page from a newspaper; ☐ a mobile.
   b) A man died ☐ in a punch-up; ☐ in hospital; ☐ on 29th April.
   c) The punch-up happened ☐ in a pub; ☐ in March; ☐ in Felton.
   d) Jack ☐ was involved in the punch-up; ☐ played cricket; ☐ was at St John's College.
   e) Jack's last text message was from ☐ a top-up phone; ☐ Janice; ☐ Rebecca; ☐ his mother
2. *Had Rebecca and Jack split up? What do YOU think?*

6 At the Red Lion

It is Friday – the day after Sergeant Draper's visit to the Red Lion. He tells Constable Briggs all about it.
Write a dialogue between the two police officers. (You can work with a partner if you like – then act it out together.)

7 That's what friends are for

1. *Can you read between the lines?*
   a) What is Lauren thinking when she says: "What happened to Jack … wasn't your fault. Not really"? (p. 25, lines 12-14)
   b) What does Samantha mean when she says: "With all your problems anyway – and now this"? (p. 27, lines 7-8)

2. *Why does Rebecca suddenly leave the café?*

3. *Is Lauren a good friend? Discuss with a partner what a 'best mate' should be like.*

8 A suspicious alibi

1. *Why is the two boys' alibi so suspicious? What does Sergeant Draper think of it?*
2. *What do the detectives want to find out from the data base?*
3. ***Something to discuss:*** *What do you think the argument between Jack and the two boys could have been about?*

9 Questions – and more questions

1. *Is this right? If anything is wrong, correct it.*

   a) Sergeant Draper offers the boys a cigarette.
   b) The police can't prove whether the cigarette ends on the cliff top were the boys' or not.
   c) Jason was given a community order in November because he was found guilty of assault and criminal damage.
   d) If Jason was involved in a serious crime again, he would be given another community order.
   e) Kevin breaks down and admits they were at the cliff top.

2. ***Things to discuss:*** *1. What might the police discover from Jason's mobile? 2. Were Jack and the two boys involved in the punch-up in Felton? Think of reasons for and against. 3. Do you think Rebecca was lying about Tuesday evening? Or might Jack have met someone else? Who could it be?*

10 The inquest

1. Flashbacks: A flashback is a scene in a story – or a film – in which we discover what happened before. The flashbacks in this chapter show Rebecca's thoughts and memories. The first one begins when she wakes up on the day of the inquest.
First decide which groups of key words belong to which flashback – and put them in a grid:

In bed: …
In the car: …
In the court: …

a) April – newspaper – dead – secret – split up
b) Jack's last day – cliff path – argument – hit – fall – motor bike – chase
c) March – trouble – someone else? – Janice?
d) Jack – cinema – Felton – pub – man – lads – kick – recognize – police?

Now use these key words to help you explain the thoughts and memories in each flashback.

2. ***Rebecca's dilemma:*** *First talk about Rebecca's thoughts and feelings before she is called to the witness box. Then decide how you think the court scene ends. (Does Rebecca tell the truth?)*

3. ***Creative writing:*** *What questions does the coroner ask Rebecca? How does she answer? (You can work with a partner for this, and then act the scene together.)*

Solutions

Before you read

a) (model answer) 1. CID detectives come and look at the body. Scene of Crime Officers look for clues and take photos. Clues are checked for fingerprints. 2. The body has to be examined by a forensic pathologist, who can find out a lot. It's important to know if it's a case of suicide.

b) 1. It shows the police that you were somewhere else and can't be the person they are looking for. 2. You make fingerprints when you put your fingers on something. Everyone has different ones. 3. If you make a confession, you talk to the police and admit what you have done. 4. We call it 'suicide' when people kill themselves. 5. People stand in the witness box when they give evidence in a court. They are asked to talk about what they've seen or what they know.

Exercises

1 On the cliffs

–

2 Detectives on the scene

1. body; 2. sergeant; 3. death; 4. helmet; 5. suspicious; 6. seat; 7. missing; 8. discovered; 9. ends; 10. suicide; 11. detectives.

3 First inquiries

1. a) Jack seemed unhappy and was worried about something. b) He was doing well at school. c) They were friends. Mark fell off the cliff when he was collecting seagulls' eggs, and was killed. d) Jack sometimes met his friends at the pub. He played cricket with them. He also had a girlfriend that he liked a lot.

4 David Briggs at work

1. He loves his work, but he finds it difficult to tell people bad news and to talk to people in shock.

2. –

5 Finding out more

a) photos of Rebecca; a page from a newspaper; b) in hospital, on 29th April. c) in March; in Felton. d) played cricket; was at St John's College. e) Rebecca.

2. –

6 At the Red Lion

–

7 That's what friends are for

1. a) "It wasn't your fault that Jack decided to end his own life, but of course, he did it because you split up with him."
   b) "I know you had problems with Jack and had split up with him, so his death must be really awful for you now."
2. She is very angry with Lauren because Lauren has told other people about her problems with Jack.
3. –

8 A suspicious alibi

1. The boys wouldn't have had enough time to go to Felton and see a film. They were seen at the Red Lion again at 9.30. Sergeant Draper calls their alibi 'rubbish'.
2. They want to find out whether the tall boy has a criminal record.
3. –

9 Questions - and more questions

1. a) He wants to find out whether they smoke. b) Fingerprints or DNA testing can prove it. c) Right. d) He might have to go to prison. e) He breaks down, but says they didn't kill Jack.
2. –

10 The inquest

1. *In bed:* c) March, etc.; d) Jack - cinema, etc.;
   In the car: a) April, etc.
   In the court: b) Jack's last day, etc.
2. –
3. –